mas
J629.8

FEB 11 2016

Winchester Public Library
Winchester, MA 01890
781-721-7171
www.winpublib.org

D1377717

ROBOT WORLD
ROBOTS IN THE FACTORY

by Jenny Fretland VanVoorst

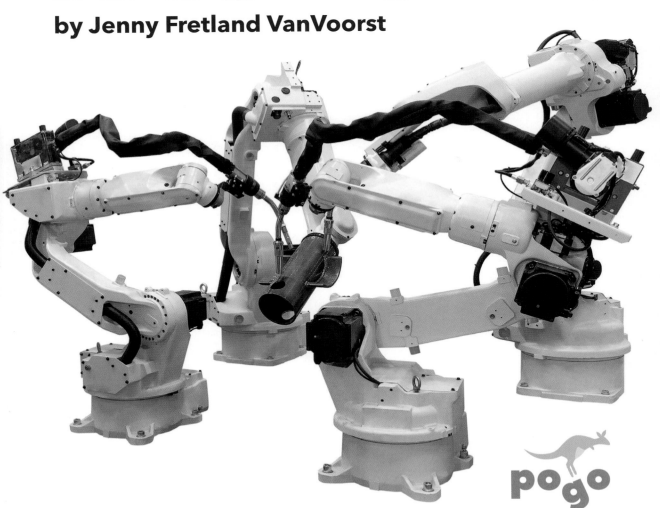

pogo

Ideas for Parents and Teachers

Pogo Books let children practice reading informational text while introducing them to nonfiction features such as headings, labels, sidebars, maps, and diagrams, as well as a table of contents, glossary, and index.

Carefully leveled text with a strong photo match offers early fluent readers the support they need to succeed.

Before Reading

- "Walk" through the book and point out the various nonfiction features. Ask the student what purpose each feature serves.
- Look at the glossary together. Read and discuss the words.

Read the Book

- Have the child read the book independently.
- Invite him or her to list questions that arise from reading.

After Reading

- Discuss the child's questions. Talk about how he or she might find answers to those questions.
- Prompt the child to think more. Ask: What do you have in your home that might have been made in a factory by a robot?

Pogo Books are published by Jump!
5357 Penn Avenue South
Minneapolis, MN 55419
www.jumplibrary.com

Copyright © 2016 Jump!
International copyright reserved in all countries.
No part of this book may be reproduced in any form without written permission from the publisher.

Library of Congress Cataloging-in-Publication Data

Fretland VanVoorst, Jenny.
 Robots in the Factory / by Jenny Fretland VanVoorst.
    pages cm. – (Robot World)
 "Pogo Books."
 Includes index.
 ISBN 978-1-62031-218-6 (hardcover: alk. paper) –
 ISBN 978-1-62496-305-6 (ebook)
 1. Robots–Juvenile literature. I. Title. II. Series
 TV211.V35 2015
 629.8'92–dc22

                                    2014005732

Series Designer: Anna Peterson
Photo Researcher: Anna Peterson

Photo Credits: All photos by Shutterstock except: Alamy, 4; Corbis, 8; Getty, 3, 14–15; iStock, 23; Science Source, 12–13, 20–21; SuperStock, 10–11, 17; Thinkstock, 5.

Printed in the United States of America at Corporate Graphics in North Mankato, Minnesota.

TABLE OF CONTENTS

· ·

CHAPTER 1

WHAT DO THEY DO?

Robots **manufacture** our world. They build our cars. They process our food. Robots in the **factory** do work that is dangerous or dull. And they do it better than people could.

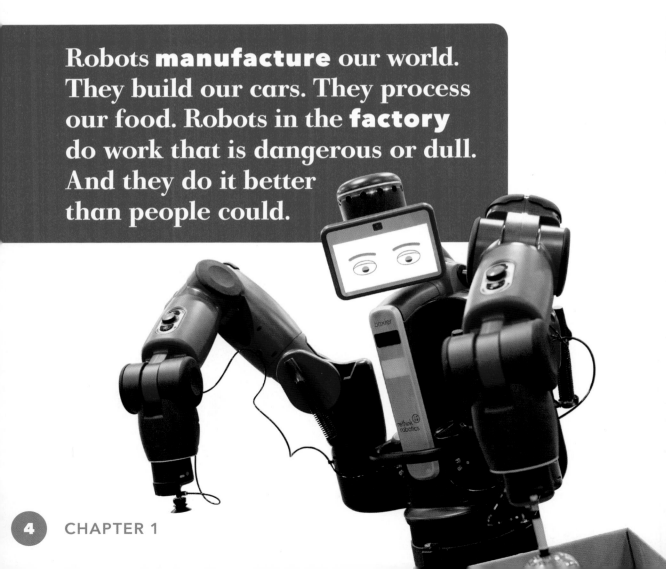

Robots always do their job perfectly. They never get bored or careless. They can work long hours. They never have to eat or sleep.

Factory robots helped build the car or bus you take to school. They cut the metal and put the parts together. They painted body panels. They moved parts from place to place.

How do robots do so many different things?

DID YOU KNOW?

The word *robot* comes from the Czech word *robota*. It means "forced labor."

CHAPTER 2

HOW DO THEY WORK?

Robots are different from a machine like your dishwasher. Dishwashers are built to do one job. But robots can do many different things.

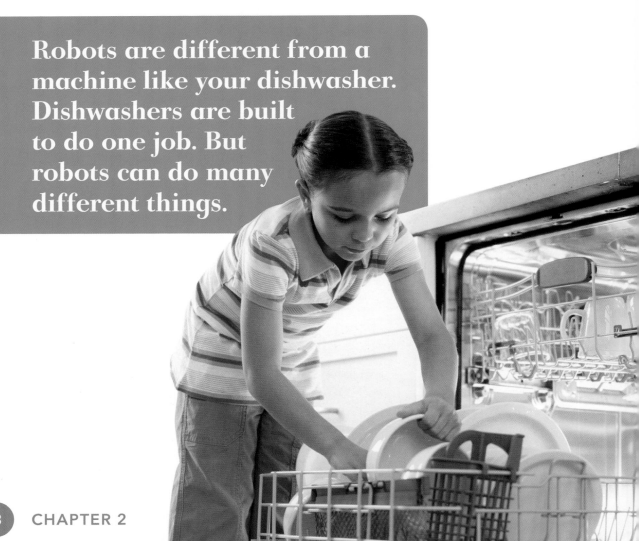

```
Filename=[Directory file name];
tic; fid=fopen(Filename); ttc=fread(fid,40); ttc=fread(fid,42);
ttc=fread(fid,inf,'1206*uint8=>uint8',58);
%ttch=dec2hex(ttc);
% Determine how many data packets.
    Packet=size(ttc)/1206;
    % Convert data to single precision.
    S1=single(ttc(2,:))*256+single(ttc(1,:));
    S2=single(ttc(102,:))*256+single(ttc(101,:));
    S3=single(ttc(202,:))*256+single(ttc(201,:));
    S4=single(ttc(302,:))*256+single(ttc(301,:));
        for i=0:10000 % Packets loop
        status(i+1)=(ttc(1205+i*1206)); value(i+1)=(ttc(1206+i*1206));
        end
        a=[85 78 73 84 35]
        fclose(fid);
        toc;
Ind=strfind(value,a);
% Loop through 64 lasers.
    for i=1:64
        temp=single(value(Ind(1)+64*(i-1)+16:Ind(1)+64*(i-1)+16+7));
        temp1=single(value(Ind(1)+64*(i-1)+32:Ind(1)+64*(i-1)+32+7));
        temp2=single(value(Ind(1)+64*(i-1)+48:Ind(1)+64*(i-1)+48+7));
        temp3=single(value(Ind(1)+64*(i-1)+64:Ind(1)+64*(i-1)+64+7));
        LaserId(i)=temp(1);
% Add high and low bytes of Vertical Correction Factor together and check if
positive or negative correction factor.
        VerticalCorr(i)=temp(3)*256+temp(2);
        if VerticalCorr(i)>32768
            VerticalCorr(i)=VerticalCorr(i)-65536;

        End
% Scale Vertical Correction Factor by Dividing by 100.
        VerticalCorr(i)=VerticalCorr(i)/100;
```

Factory robots work off of **programs**. Programs can be changed. They can be replaced by other programs.

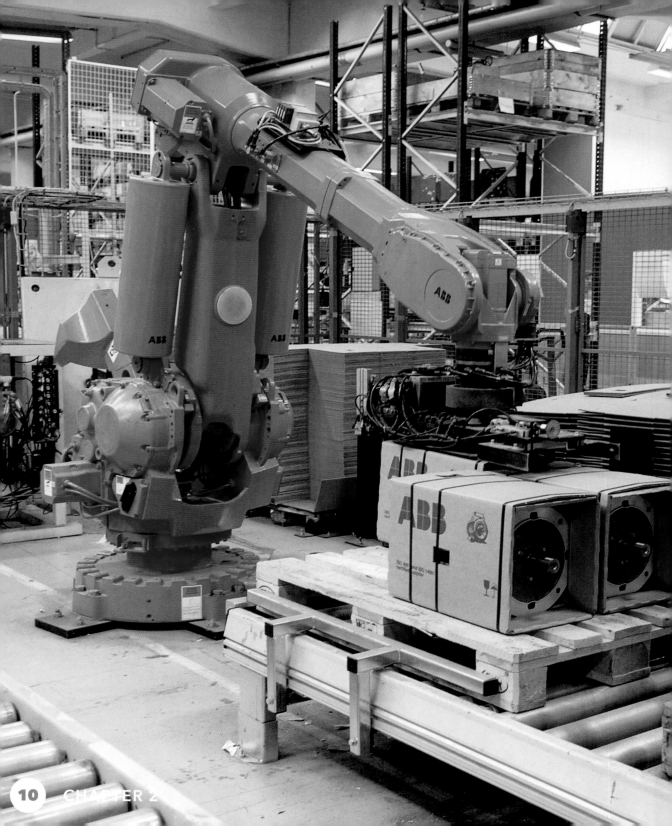

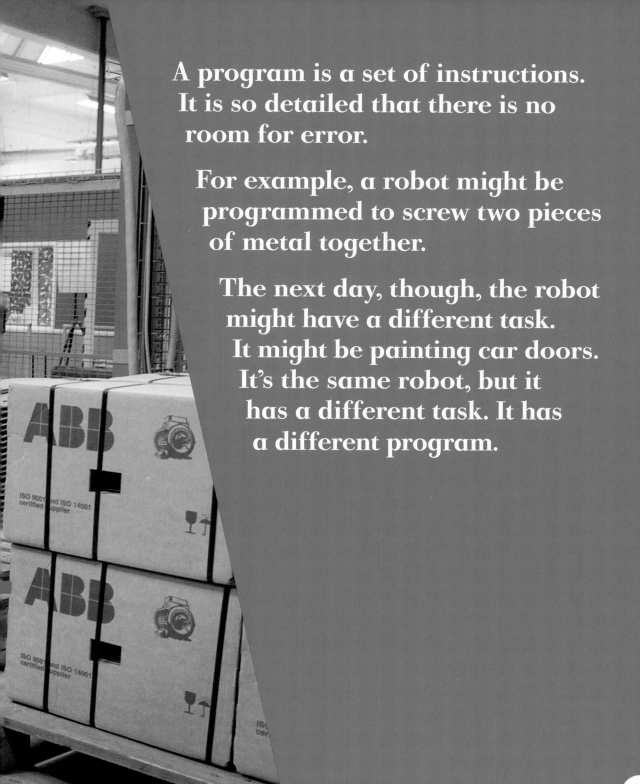

A program is a set of instructions. It is so detailed that there is no room for error.

For example, a robot might be programmed to screw two pieces of metal together.

The next day, though, the robot might have a different task. It might be painting car doors. It's the same robot, but it has a different task. It has a different program.

To carry out its program, a robot must be able to move. It might have an arm that can grasps things. Or it could have wheels that allow it to move from place to place.

In order to move within its world, it needs to know what its world looks like. Every robot has tools that help it make sense of its surroundings. These tools are called **sensors**. They are like a robot's eyes and ears. Sensors can be cameras, microphones, and **GPS**. They can be **lidar** and **radar**. They can be heat or pressure sensors.

Let's look at a few factory robots.

sensors

CHAPTER 3

MEET THE ROBOTS

Most factory robots are used to build cars.

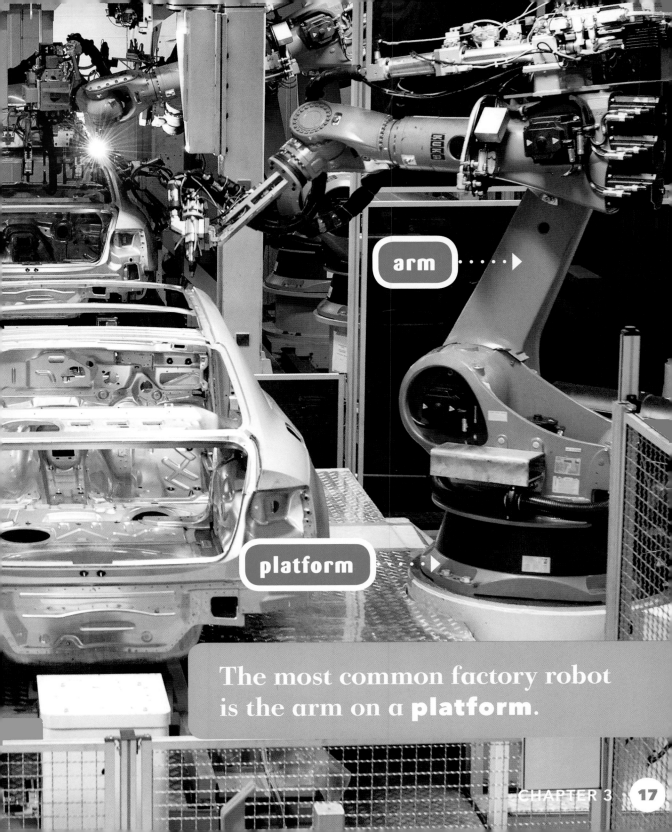

arm

platform

The most common factory robot is the arm on a **platform**.

There are nearly a million and a half robots in use in factories worldwide.

WHERE ARE THEY?

TOP 10 COUNTRIES BY ROBOT DENSITY

Country	Robot Density
Japan	295
Singapore	169
South Korea	164
Germany	163
Sweden	126
Italy	124
Finland	98
Belgium	89
U.S.A.	86
Spain	84

Industrial robots per 10,000 human factory workers

Some companies with large **warehouses** use robots to bring items to workers. A central computer controls traffic. Each robot takes the fastest route. None gets in the way of another.

So many things in our lives have been built by a robot. Look around. What has a robot made for you?

ACTIVITIES & TOOLS

PROGRAM A ROBOT

Turn your friend into a robot! If you do a good job, you may end up with a tasty snack!

What You Need:
- peanut butter
- two slices of bread
- jam or jelly (optional)
- butter knife
- pencil and paper

❶ Write down the steps needed to make a peanut butter sandwich. Then ask a friend to follow the steps exactly, without taking anything for granted or making any assumptions.

❷ For example, it is not enough to ask your friend to reach for the peanut butter. How far should she extend her arm? Should she angle it up or down? How much? When should she grasp the jar? When should she let go?

❸ How far did your friend get before there was a problem? Record the error and replan. Then rewrite the instructions, and try again.

factory: A place where products are made by hand or machinery.

GPS: A navigation system that uses satellite signals to find the location of a radio receiver on or above the earth's surface; abbreviation of global positioning system.

lidar: A device that uses laser beams to detect and locate objects.

manufacture: To make products by hand or machinery.

platform: A level, raised surface that keeps a robot stable and in place.

program: A set of instructions that a robot follows.

radar: A device that uses radio waves to detect and locate objects.

sensors: Onboard tools that serve as a robot's eyes, ears, and other sense organs so that the robot can create a picture of the environment in which it operates.

warehouse: A large building where manufactured items are stored.

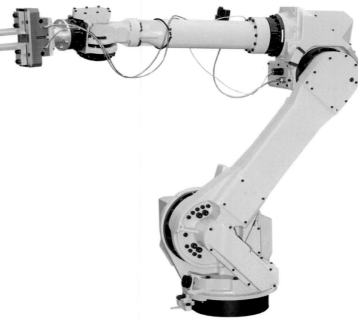

INDEX

TO LEARN MORE

Learning more is as easy as 1, 2, 3.

1) Go to www.factsurfer.com

2) Enter "robotsinthefactory" into the search box.

3) Click the "Surf" to see a list of websites.

With factsurfer, finding more information is just a click away.